West of the Santa Ana
and Other Sacred Places

West of the Santa Ana
and Other Sacred Places

DIOSA XOCHIQUETZALCÓATL

RIOT OF ROSES
PUBLISHING HOUSE
SEJATNGA
UNCEDED TONGVA TERRITORY
SOUTH WHITTIER, CALIFORNIA

Published by Riot of Roses Publishing House

West of the Santa Ana and Other Sacred Places
Copyright © 2023, Adriana Citlali Brenes-Rios
ISBN: 978-1-961717-00-8 (paperback)
ISBN: 978-1-961717-01-5 (ebook)
Library of Congress Control Number: 2023940305

First Edition, 2023

Printed in the United States of America.

www.riotofrosespublishinghouse.com

Cover art by T'sanda Janini.
Cover design work by Riot of Roses Publishing House.
Edited by Brenda Vaca.
Interior book design by Brenda Vaca.

ADVANCE PRAISE

Diosa Xochiquetzalcóatl is a poet that brings history, culture, and scars to the party of new beginnings. Every poem is the sound of laughter and tears, evoking courage to move past barriers, comfort, and fear, building new homes from old shadows that always protect us as long as we bring them to the party.

Ceasar K. Avelar, Author of *God of The Air Hose And Other Blue-Collar Poems*, and Poet Laureate of Pomona.

Diosa's poems in *West of the Santa Ana and other Sacred Places*, is an InLakech between pages leading us to notice basuritas out in the alleyways of So-Cal, as well as bring voice to the ghosts of the citrus fields of North Orange County labored by Mexican and Native hands. Sweet memories of orange grooves are spell-casted in the naming of "invisible borderlands," "mexican panaderias," and "tent-city galore." The reader may taste the mist of tequila rhymes, MEChistA rage, and the airy waters of Southern California's largest natural river, the Santa Ana river. Diosa's poems are her very own mélange of fierce feminine thunder over cacti.

Iuri M. Lara

West of The Santa Ana and Other Sacred Places doesn't stand still. Este libro es poesía en marcha. Her third collection of poetry is a call to follow Diosa through time and landmarks not specific to any map with defined latitude and longitude. Diosa's poems are a perpetual movement of emotion and place. Start at the beginning and visit the dream she was born of and the ancestral memory carried in our DNA. Run through dichos, children's songs, and the shadows of the very real Cucuy lurking in the neighborhoods that Diosa's poetic soul lives in. Discover how anger can travel through the womb and let love catch you on the other side of a poem.

This third book allows the reader to experience Diosa's miracle, the many dimensions of heart, body and soul. The portal to Diosa Dimension is *West of the Santa Ana and Other Sacred Places*.

Aideed Medina, Author of *31 Hummingbird*, Xingao Press

As someone who is from west of the Santa Ana River, I enjoy voices that speak of this river. Diosa Xochiquetzalcóatl narrates how she went with the flow, which led her northeast of the Santa Ana River to Rancho Paraíso de Las Diosas, where nature is let be. Diosa once made a place further west of the Santa Ana home, known for its mall and buses that travel into near La Habra (closer to Santa Ana River) and Downtown LA. *West of the Santa Ana And Other Sacred Places* teaches that it's okay to migrate to polar horizontal opposites of the Santa Ana, and it's okay not to be destined to be rooted. As Diosa continues to flow east and west of the Santa Ana, she lets us know we should share a grain with one another in this sacred world because water is what unites us all.

Jesse Tovar, Editor, Lit Stack, litstack.substack.com

Diosa takes us on a viaje suave through herstory with precision and lyrical prowess. Generational curses, love of place, and vocal chakras made me laugh and nod with approval of facts and remembrance. This short collection of poems is to be read out loud and shared.

Edward Vidaurre, Author of *Cry, Howl* and *Pandemia & Other Poems*

Diosa's poetry takes us to a place called home – where she recalls the beauty of "brown pride" and what it is like to be a Mexican living in Guada La Habra, just west of Santa Ana. She recalls the panaderias and her tia Consuelo's homemade flour tortillas, the Mexican families that live by the railroads, the migrant farmworkers nestled among the groves of citrus trees.

Her voice is one of an activist, a feminist, a womanist and her characters reject misogyny and patriarchal expectations as they say no to marriage and no to domestic duties, as if expressing, "A la fregada con esas cosas" and clearly saying goodbye to all the "suckas," men who failed the strong, independent, female narrator.

Furthermore, Diosa treads on the personal and confessional, and reflects on the "faulty lines" of love, on the ever-changing emotions of love. She bares her soul and writes about the "tumultuous thunders of your love. /Your walloping winds carried me away/ while your rapid rains flooded my barren canyons." These lines are raw, powerful, and honest and it is refreshing for a writer to reveal this vulnerability. We empathize with her sadness and heartbreak.

Her poetry makes me feel like I want to sit in a porch with Diosa with a cold drink of homemade Jamaica or Horchata and listen to all of her stories on a Sunday afternoon. Because her poetry, the narrative, and the characters recall real and genuine individuals that have lived with us.

Her poetry reminds us that even though Mexican families are prey to gentrification and the changing environment, that raza, our gente are still here, thriving and surviving.

Diosa reminds me of this with some of my favorite lines, which are a testimonial metaphor of this brilliant collection – "El Campo lives forever in the hearts and minds of gold/ as long as we keep retelling these stories never told." Diosa has written about our people's resiliency with beauty. We are here!

Professor Donato Martinez, Author of *Touch the Sky*

Table of Contents

Westward Ho!

Eastward Expansion

The Wanderer

EL PREFACE

My Poems Are Like Pictures

They capture moments in time.
Sometimes good.
Sometimes not.
Some are portraits of timeless stories,
while others are merely fading snapshots.

WESTWARD

HO!

Rancho Cañada de La Habra

A Valley Unknown

¡Guada-La Habra! ¡Guada-La Habra!
¡Guada-La Habra! ¡Guada-La Habra!

"Tienes el alma más mexicana...." *
gratas memorias de esta Xicana.

-my first step
-my first pet
-the place where I first felt regret.

La Habra — the opening, in ancient Castilian.
Pleiadian portal of light beings, most certainly, not reptilian.
(Despite Nixon's first law office, of course.)

The valley between *La Puente* and Fullerton's Coyote Hills.
Mid-point for enlightened ancestors
and childish tricksters looking for thrills.

The invisible borderlands between the great O.C.
and L.A. County's vast and varied diversity.

¡Ay, ay, ay! ¡Arriba Unión de Tula!
Where everyone seemed related, except for this lil' chula.

Where Adriana was always "ah-dr-yah-nah,"
not a slaughtered "ey-dree-ana."
A citruss-covered valley, in no way, a barren savannah.

The Corn Festival parades that ended at *El Centro* Park.
O.L.G.'s Annual *Fiestas* that always got hotter after dark.

---

*   Melody and quote from the Mexican mariachi song, *Guadalajara.*

"Hands Across America" down Whittier in the 4th grade.
The Gary Center and Rosie's Garage,
where beautiful dreams were made.
The interactive Children's Museum, first of only a few.
A place where you knew everyone and everyone knew you.

Barbara's notorious palm readings and psychic premonitions.
Margarita's garage-made-studio, fashion designer creations.

Disney's spectacular firework's show which was really not that far.
ER visit due to *Valencia* Elementary's misfortunate monkey bar.

The Zappster Twins. *El Pájaro Nalgón.*
Our *chicote*-wearing *quebradita* crew—*chingón.*

Jimmy Quack-Quack *y La Joyona.*
Radio's iconic Jimmy Reyes live and in persona.

Home of the famous "Brown Pride" ride.
El Campo—a place filled with Mexican pride.

Ditching parties and hickies on Grace.
Highlanders vs. Raiders—never-ending high school race.

Twisted ankles and posadas off Pacific.
24-hour runs to *Taquería De Anda ¡que* terrific!

Bus rides to the ocean down that oh-so-famous Beach,
then down Harbor Blvd. for that higher education reach.

Nothing will ever beat its authentic, Mexican *panaderías*
nor my *tía* Consuelo's *cocido* and homemade flour *tortillas.*

Guada-La Habra...

A valley unknown.
A place I called home.

El Campo

"Naranja dulce, limón partido. Dame un abrazo, que yo te pido.
Si fueran falsos mis juramentos, en otros tiempos se olvidarán...""

Citrus groves of the past.
Mexican families by the railroad tracks.

Migrant farmworkers from Pixley and beyond.
Chicana Jilguerillas sing their melodious songs.

El Chicano Fermín, the talk of the town.
Tramping on trains is how peeps got around.

The Sunkist Association. Tent-city galore.
The Standard Oil Company, bringing in more and more.

As the city crowded in, the *campesinos* faded out.
Hardly anyone is left for us to even talk about.

Gone are the fruit-bearing *huertos* of a city's yesteryear.
The original *Campo de La Habra* has, quite almost, disappeared.

A story once forgotten. Perhaps, a story never known.
A story purposefully left out, erasing *Raza* from their home.

El Campo lives forever in the hearts and minds of gold
as long as we keep retelling these stories never told.

"Toca la marcha. Mi pecho llora. Adiós señora, yo ya me voy
a mi casita de sololoy a comer tacos y no le doy."

---

*   *Naranja dulce* is a traditional Mexican children's song.

The Yesterdays of Today

Monkey bars, sand in my face
Large fields of tall, bug-filled weeds
Sour grass with tiny yellow flowers
Recess and classrooms at *Valencia*

Moving to another school
Because mine was closed down
Maypole dance at *Ladera Palma*
Pastel–colored ribbons and bows
Right behind the classroom
Next to *Loma Norte* Park

My dad
Victim of militarization
Drafted to Nam
All the way from Mexico City
Fighting for a country
That fought against his own
Trail of Tears
Cherokee Nation
Undocumented natives
Due to *wasichu* laws

Mamá
Mexican-born descendant of a US citizen
"No naturalization papers for you!"
Who couldn't breathe in the U.S.
Yet became the exemplary housewife
Embodying the typical American
Consumeristic and capitalistic home

Protests, letters, and bumper stickers
Walk in defiance
Devil's advocate
Do not abide by the status quo
Do not abide by the status quo
DO NOT ABIDE BY THE STATUS QUO
Question
Decolonize
Embrace
Cultura—la tuya

THERE ONCE WAS A LITTLE BOY

Who lived in this little city.
Who was befriended by an evil man.
Who didn't come home one day.
Who didn't come home the next day either.

Days later, a brick appeared.
And the next day, another.
Until all the scattered bricks
spread throughout this tiny city
were pieced together.

There once was a little a boy
who finally came home.*

---

*   In memory of Juan Delgado (1998).

CHIPS

Cuando de pequeña yo lloraba,
mi mamá me decía
"!Oy! Oye al Chips.
¿Dónde está Chips?"

Mi perro
choco-chispeado
ladraba y ladraba
mientras yo
lloraba y lloraba
hasta que yo me cansaba,
él también.

Choco-chispas.
Hasta la fecha,
entre chispas de chocolate
encuentro mi confort.
He llorado y llorado
y mis choco-chispas
me han confortado
hasta agotarnos los dos.

My Besties

I met Maggie
at the age of three.
Her grandparents
didn't speak Spanish.
My Mexican mother
didn't speak English,
and neither of us
spoke much of either.
We were the
OG Rugrats
of the great O.C.

In kindergarten,
I met Martha.
I ended up in her house
one day after school
because I guess
I was allowed
to walk myself home
at the age of five.

After coming home
with two gifts:
a tattered doll
and a head full of lice,
I wasn't allowed
to be her friend
anymore.

I met Lucy
at the bus stop
on the first day
of first grade.
Her parents
spoke Spanish
like mine,
but I don't think
we ever spoke it.
Her humongous yard
made for endless hours
where forests, jungles,
and safaris came to life.

I don't remember
when I met Elena
even though we grew up
in the same neighborhood.
But I do remember,
she was a *traviesa*.
Wads of wet paper
stuck to the ceilings
of boring bathrooms
where Bloody Marys
would come to life.

...And then I moved
to the other side of town.

The Other Side of Town

That's where I met Lora, Vero, and the Twins.
And I think we met in that same order.
And that's the same order I would pick them up
on my way to school.

Lora, Vero and I,
we'd tell each other ghost stories
in the dark and empty church
while ditching catechism.

The Twins and I,
we almost got run over
right in front of *La Taquería de Anda*.
Well, the only one who would have
been made a *tortilla* was me
because the Twins had already run
back to the sidewalk, screaming.

I still see Lora and the Twins.
Vero, not so much, not really.

But for many years, they were,
and will forever be, my besties.

Hearts on Fire

I was just a little girl
when Jesus came to visit
on the night of the full moon,
perfect night for Holy Spirit.

Jesus and his apostles,
their hearts were set aflame.
And when I looked up to the sky,
the moon had done the same.

As I opened up my little eyes,
I thought I'd gone insane.
A burning in my heart—colossal.
The moon, on fire, remained.

The dream crept into my world.
I found myself living within it.
Panicked, I ran to my parents' room.
Yet my parents seemed not to worrit.

I cried in bed throughout the night.
Paralyzed by this gruesome sight
the night that Jesus and his apostles
showed up in my room to visit.

BROOM HILDA

Picture it.
The year was 1981
in a little city
at the tippy-top of Orange County.

A little girl by the name of Hilda
was being trained to be
a good, little homemaker
—some man's wife,
if she was lucky!

And so she was taught
how to sweep the floors,
make the beds,
do the laundry,
take out the trash,
polish the furniture,
and set the table.

But, little did the adults know
que a Hilda, ¡le barrieron los pies!

That's right!
Hilda's sister had swept her feet
one time when they played house.

Since that glorious moment,
something inside her
went tick-tock-kaboom.

From then on,
Hilda hated domestic chores
and anything confined to a room.

She abhorred the floors,
the laundry and beds.
She detested the house;
preferred the outdoors instead.

When it came to cutting the grass
and raking up the debris,
she was in her own *bruja* heaven
(if there is even such a thing.)

She would conjure up potions
with grass cuttings and leaves,
cast up spells with worms and ants,
and even talk to trees.

She began to rhyme
and dance in time
with the winds, the birds, and the bees.

She'd bend her body
in all sorts of ways
replacing her feet with her knees.

And the more that she grew,
she loathed the idea
of having to say, "I do."

And now in book three,
it dawned on me
why the conventional made her so blue.

Hilda and the broom
had become a solid pair,
leaving no room for a groom.

Broom Hilda is her name,
brujería is her game,
y con la escoba, ella vuela. Zoom! Zoom!

A Mathematician's Antithesis

Mrs. P
passed her test
by bubbling in
a witch.

For a girl
hating Math,
this was music
to ears.

Ms. B.-R.
passed her test
by bubbling in
a witch.

So, they taught
all, but Math,
for many years.
The end.

The "Good-Ole" American Sentence

You Chicanos are a bunch of lowlifes and belong out on the streets!

Signed,

Middle School Substitute
(circa 1990)

Go Raiders!

blue and gold
[water][colors]
a Sonora High School memory

Empanadas de Calabaza

She pulled me out of an *agavachada* kitchen.
Save the pumpkins! Save the pumpkins!
Say no to Jack-O-Lanterns.

She pulled out of the *calabaza* the same seeds
I would buy at the corner liquor store.
The same seeds!

She pulled me into a Mexican kitchen
where I learned to knead the *masa*, cook the *calabaza*,
bake the *empanada*, then eat them with my *Nana*.

She pulled and pulled and pulled the *mexicana*,
the same one my mom tried to stuff away
en las empanadas de mi Nana.*

---

* This poem first appeared online on the Círculo de poetas & Writers website, 2022.

Prayer Warrior

My momma is a prayer warrior.
That's what my shaman friend did say.
While I protested, defended, and marched,
she'd stay at home to pray.

My mother is not a fighter.
She keeps arguments at bay.
She keeps her rosary in hand,
where, forever, it will stay.

"Tú que tienes palancas con Chuyito,"
I requested her help one day.
My problems soon dissolved
as she prayed for my dismay.

My momma is a prayer warrior
stronger than *Opus Dei*,
a *Guadalupana, hueso colorado.*
with sainthood on the way.

My momma, the prayer warrior,
the one who made me the woman and the Goddess I am today.

MARCHITA

Se marchitó mi Margarita,[*]
hermana, madre, tía y abuelita.
Ya se fue para el otro mundo,
como el cuento de la "one" mariposita.

Ella ya no podía volar,
pues anclada estaba a su camita.
Se le acabó el recorrido mundano
a una bella y fuerte damita.

Sus pétalos se fueron cayendo
uno por uno con certeza.
Ya la muerte dominaba
aquella, su gran fortaleza.

No se puede evitar
lo que dicta la naturaleza.
Se marchitó mi Margarita,
llenando mi jardín de tristeza.

---

[*]   In memory of Margarita Ríos Hernández, 1926-2022.

Imperial Burgers

It was the spot,
THE burger joint of L.H.,
the after-party party spot,
be it sports games or kickbacks,
school dances or clubs,
family outings or dates,
lazy summers or
munchy winters.

Even in 2022,
after my grandma's
mortuary services,
the night ended there.

It was the spot;
it still is the spot;
and it will always be.

The Search

My elders have always been looking for me ever since I was a child.
They all poured into the city in the 80's,
when I was still in elementary school:
my sister, my brother, and my lover.
But I was so young then, they did not know it was me.

My sister would visit my little city all the time
because her mother lived there.
I'm sure we crossed paths at St. Vincent De Paul.

My brother, he made my hometown his hometown
on his way from *Guatemala.*
I have no doubt that we bumped shopping carts at Northgate.

My lover took his girls to the school at OLG.
And I'll be damned if he wasn't picking them up
while I was being dropped off
or if he wasn't driving out while we were driving in.

On Monday nights, we went to *el grupo de oración,*
where people would drop like flies and *Anita* spoke in tongues.

In the middle of the week, (I can't remember what day,
and neither could my mom because she would always forget
to pick us up) there was catechism.

On Saturday mornings, I was my grandma's teacher's aide
for her Kindergarten *clase de catesismo.*

And every Sunday morning, we'd arrive for *la misa de las 7:45*
at 7 ante-(fuckin')-meridian!

30-some years later, the search was over.
My sister, my brother, and my lover found me
far away from this city of mine.

My sister had introduced me to my brother.
My brother had introduced me to my lover.
And once the lessons were learned,
we all went our separate ways.

In the Great O.C.

El movimiento de Fullerton

I was a MEChistA.
Era una chispa, una mecha de verdad,
cantando con mariachi con trajes de Adelita en cada movimiento cultural.

Adela López, Jerry Padilla, and "Kiki" Zúñiga by our side.
Kindercaminata. Adelante Mujer. Fullerton College was my pride.

I was a MEChistA.
Reformista. Progresista. Una mecha sin parar.
Yo fui. Yo soy. Y yo siempre seré MEChistA hasta el final.

The Santa Ana River

The river took me away from my hometown.
It took me far away.
And now in book three, it wants me to come back.
It wants me to come home and stay.

I think it heard my mother pray.

But I am a *Ríos*, destined by nature.
I am meant to go with the flow.
To run through lakes and creeks and rivers.
To touch the oceans, I must always go.

Earth is more than 70% water.
Hence, the planet, I must roam.
I may come from the city of *La Habra*.
But this entire planet is my home.

El Pueblo de Nuestra Señora La Reina de Los Ángeles de Porciúncula

Saturday Morning rancheras at Church

Preach, I say! Preach!

Teach us the way of the word!
Your word, my word, our words,
the written channelings of our Higher Power
—those meant to destroy and devour
the monsters in our head,
—those designed to heal as we reveal
the wounds hidden under bed.

The 10 ethics, our 10 commandments.
Captains, caretakers, and co-pilots.

C - I see you.
L - I love you.
I - ¡Ay, ay, ay!
Jose Alfredo Jiménez, ¡trucha!

We are the bloodletting *rancheras*
that sing along to the *qui-qui-ri-qui* of the cocks.

To the women, the children, the elders, and men,
my beloved brothers and sisters, a-**womb**-men!*

---

*   To my Saturday morning CLI-que, this one's for you.

¡PINCHES MARGARITAS!

Let's stop drinking *margaritas* and calling them lemonade!

This ain't no walk in the park
with butterflies and flutterflies,
cute little rainbows, nor pink hearts.

This is a combination of sweet and sour.
And all the *pinches vasos están todos* salty.

This shit is on the rocks!
No steady, solid ground.
Full of rough and tumble,
crash and crumble.

Ching, cling,
shake, rattle and roll,
and down, down, DOWN, we go.

Nah, this ain't no rutti-tutti,
fresh and fruity.
Fuck no!

Hard gulps of burning liquor
that not only impair my judgment in the now,
but continue to fuck with my head the next morning.
SHIT! But they taste so fucking good!

Unlike lemonade,
which brings peaceful pleasure to the palette,
THIS brings wasted nights
and lingering hangovers
that last for more than a tomorrow.

What a cruel addiction **THIS** is!
Knowing that it is bad for my health,
but I – just – can't – get – **ENOUGH!**
¡Basta! ¡Ya estuvo!

Yeah, right.
I hear the tinkling of ice cubes in my empty cup,
and my mouth begins to water.

Fucken' ey!
The *margaritas* in L.A.

What else can I say?!

POR AHÍ

Aquella ciudad que no puedo mencionar

Esa casa
      Esa recamara
            Donde hicimos el amor
                  Donde nos vinimos a la misma vez
                        Donde querías que me quedara para siempre

Aunque no la pueda mencionar, la recuerdo

The Girl Who Likes to Visit Parks Late at Night

Highland

Monterey

    Arroyo Seco

    San Pascual

        Baldwin

        Ascot Hills

            Huntington

            Los Ángeles State Historic

Too many memories to write in just one poem

So Long Suckas

Because of all the assholes living in L.A.,
I definitely should move closer to the bay.
People in NorCal—friendly, they say.
Perchance up North, I will see much a-brighter-day.
Maybe in a lake, I'll catch a nice fellow, I pray.
I'm sick of all these L.A. *putos* who just love to play.
I must, I could, I should and would, certainly today,
leave behind the many assholes living in L.A.

P.S.
To the
(two-one-three),
(six-two-six),
(three-two-three),
and (five-six-two),
any which way I dial you up,
so long suckas, we're through!

CRUISIN'

CROSSROADS

She was the 60 fwy, and they, the 605.

The one to the North,
the land of the ancestors,
was a younger fellow.

The one to the South,
the land of the children,
was an older man.

Both from the land of Mictlán.
Both, masters of darkness.

She now stands on the overpass
with obsidian sphere in hands,
clearly seeing the mirrored lessons
through the thick L.A. County smoke.

She had stretched her right arm to the South.
She had stretched her left arm to the North.

Only to have been crucified at the crossroads of the 60 and the 605.

MEMORY LANE

Fucking GPS!
You just had to bring me here, I guess!

Out of all the damn streets in Southern California,
you had to take me down Memory Lane
in some type of masochistic confrontation
of apparent unhealed pain.

Son of a bitch!
What the hell does (562) have to do with (714)?!
Listen to the raven's echo whisper, "Nevermore!"

Each street,
each corner,
each turn,
a drop,
filling my cup
until my cup could no longer be contained.

Pinche Memory Lane!
Who would've thought that after all these years
you could still bring so much pain!

MONTEBELLO

Entre cerros serenos

Montebello
bello monte,
bellos momentos,
bellos recuerdos.

Recuerdo mis domingos
llenos de alegría,
llenos de familia,
llenos de risas y comida.
Las niñas y los niños jugábamos
mientras los adultos platicaban y bebían.

No importaba
que en la casa de mi tía
no cupiera ni su propia plebada,
nosotr@s felices en la yarda
entre el humo de Marlboros
y el aroma de la carne asada.

Montebello,
bello monte,
bellos momentos,
bellos recuerdos.

I've Got Two Lovers

I met them both
in *Montebello*
in the time of the best full moons
when wolves are on the prowl.
Ahhhh-ooooohhhh!

Happy birth month to me!
Happy birth month, indeed!

Neither of them
were from
el bello monte
of *Montebello,*
yet that is where their
physical manifestation
occurred.

Near the *Juan Matías Sánchez Adobe*.
Near the *Río Hondo* Channel.

And as a well-rounded Libra,
I got two, and I ain't ashamed!

MARAVILLA

OUR LADY OF MAGDALA

Our Lady of Solitude, why are you lonely?
Doth not the Lord sayeth, "Do not fear, for I am with you?"*

Our Lady of Solitude, why do you shed tears?
Doth not the Lord sayeth, "I will strengthen you and help you?"

Our Lady of Solitude, why are you forsaken?
Doth not the Lord sayeth, "Do not be dismayed,
for I am your God?"

Could it be that you have uncovered the truth?

Could it be that you have seen how our women and children
have been tarnished at the hands of these "fathers"?

Could it be that you've grown weary
of the patriarchal practices of your church?

I, too, have wept.
I, too, have felt betrayed and alone.
That is exactly why I built "A Church of My Own."

Dry your tears and be moved into action from all this pain
in the Goddess's name.
A-**womb**-men.

---

*   From Isaiah 41:10

The HEARTS of Maravilla

Gota. Gotita.
Drip. Drop.
On the streets of *Cesar Chavez* Avenue,
the neon signs light up the paved corridors of *Maravilla*.
The best of *caldos de pollo* and *panes dulces*
heal achy bodies and help people make peace with their *penas*.
Our Lady of Solitude
comforts the lonely Christians at Christmas time.
And Tonalli Studios brings the he**ARTS** to life
and life to loving he**ARTS**.

Rancho Paraíso de las Diosas

HUITZI

Little hummingbird
Huitzilipochtli
The one that flies to the left

Tzintzun

Vuela colibrí
Ave de mil colores
Vuela sin parar

THE WINGED CREATURES ARE HAPPY

The blue jays
the butterflies
the hummingbirds
the dragonflies

joyous they hop
content they fly

in their magical queendom
Rancho Paraíso de las Diosas

CEREMONY CON EL ZORRILLO

full moon / dark night
sacred smoke / black and white

Flower emerges from *entre las flores*
Flower *se aparece detrás* the smokey veil

blanco y negro / black and white
the juxtaposition of my life

en español, primero la luz
in English, darkness comes first

a black and white skunk
at the forefront of a black sky and white moon

populated solitude / distant proximity
sola in the physical, but in the *más allá, ni se diga*

close enough to see / far too far to touch
the oxymoron of my life

a skunk that's black, but white
a sky that's dark, but bright
ceremony *con el zorrillo*
in the still of the night

En mi rancho

Entre coyotes y gatitas,
zorillos y tlacuaches,
danzamos bajo la luna.

Entre pasiflora y rositas,
jacarandas y noches buenas,
danzamos bajo el sol.

Entre cristales y calaveras,
veladoras y copal,
cantamos bajo la luna.

Entre tambores y sonajas,
extraños ruidos en la casa,
cantamos y danzamos con todo el corazón.

Bienvenid@s al Rancho Paraíso de las Diosas.

THE 951

La casa de Jurupa

La casa que pudo haber sido de la pareja
que tuvo miedo enamorarse.

La veo, entre carros y carretera, a diario.
Un recordatorio de lo que pudo haber sido, pero nunca lo será.

RIVERSIDE CONVENTION CENTER

The phone rang early the next morning.
A momma was looking for her (adult) baby boy.

Le dije que lo había secuestrado,
que su baby era mi chiquibaby
a quien me llevé de parranda
la noche anterior
a ver a mis amores,
Los Tiranos y Monchis
y que después del zapateado
había seguido la zarandeada,
y que nos disculpara
muchísimo
porque aún nos faltaba el mañanero.

Click.

San Andreas

Faulty Love Lines

My love is for, but a season.
Passionate one morning, tepid the next day.
Without rhyme; without reason.
Listens to no one; follows its own way.

It is San Andreas's fault.
For it is neither here nor there.
There's a crevice that runs deep.
That seemingly ends nowhere.

My emotions run to the North.
My thoughts linger to the South.
Neither joining force.
Filling me with doubt.

My love is for, but a season.
Ever-changing, every day.
Without rhyme; without reason.
And itinerant it will stay.

La falla de San Andrés

¿Cuál es la gran falla de San Andrés?
El haber retado a su Santa Micaela.

HARK!

A southern gust rushed in at the haunting hour!

A roaring rumble streaked through the midnight sky!

Then, there came the rolling of the ground

as the masses were left to die.

DOWN BY THE RIVER

surrounded by water
in the beginning
Atl'antix
Lumeria
Tenochtitlan
turtle emerges
from deep blue sea
to give us this
our island
in the womb
we grow
to the sway
of amniotic fluid
fluir
como los rios
como la sangre
my blood flows
my tears flow
my dreams float
on the surface
of a lake
exposed
with nowhere to go
because man
has damned
the rivers

Alta California

La California Jackpot

Jackpot!
Seems you found the girl that hits your spot!

Cha-ching! Cha-ching!
You've located my bell, now let it ring.
Seems to be your favorite thing.

¡Te ganaste el premio mayor!
Sure played your cards right, *señor.*

Le pegaste al gordo, o mejor dicho,
le pegaste duro a la gordita,
dulce y redondita
como esas dos cerecitas.

Your very own scratcher,
to scratch and sniff.

You just simply get a whiff
and you drop to your knees
like James Brown, begging, "Please, baby, please!"
Gotcha smiling so much bigger than when you say, "Cheese!"

¡HEH-HEH-HEH!
¡Pos' órale!
Al pan, pan y al vino, vino.
No cabe duda, que te sacaste la lotería conmigo.

May the odds be ever in your favor
because if this romance ever waivers,
unlike me, your pain will be graver.

So, don't throw all your chips in the pot
because you may not end up knowing
how to handle this California Jackpot.

NORMALCY

Amber alerts resume to light up freeway signs.
A 73% increase in L.A.'s violent crimes.
Record-breaking heat waves fill this summertime.

Congratulations, Californians!
"We are dying to get back to normal!" you panted.
So now, your wish has been dutifully granted.
N'est pas?

My Favorite Californian Café

My ex would have died up in here.

Where all the cowboys and cowgirls meet.
Where biker gangs and Trumpers eat.

But I'm a down-to-earth, hippie-dippie girl
who loves to people-watch to understand the world.

I sit and eat my all-American breakfast
while listening to country tunes.

When leaving, monster trucks and motorcycles
intoxicate me with their fumes.

Confederate flags and "make America great"
fill up most of the café.

Yet, my confident, brown-skinned presence
leaves them with nothing to say.

This place isn't located in the deep South yonder.
Just close enough to where I live to make me sit and ponder…

Oh, how my ex would have died up in here!

Piñata Party in SoCal

He was way too close for comfort,
especially for a little girl
who was already afraid of the dark.

They called him the Night Stalker.
And right before the summer of '85,
the attack in Whittier
was just a skip away.

My brother would scare the shit out of us
by recounting the stupid stories he'd heard on the news.
Then mama would yell, "¡Ya cállate y vete a dormir!"
Then papa would yell, "¿Ya cerraron todas las ventanas?"
We had to sleep with our windows sealed shut and one eye open.

It was the longest summer ever, sleeping through soaked pjs.
IDK if it was sweat due to the heat or the paranoia!
Or maybe the fear made me pee my pants every night.
Neta que no sé.
But it was a hell of a summer.

Then, on August 31st, breaking news.
Raza in East L.A. had spotted the serial killer.
"Dale, dale, dale. No pierdas el tino.*
Porque si lo pierdes" SE ESCAPA EL ASESINO.
¡Y le dieron una paliza, que pa' que te cuento!
Tanto, tanto that reports say the puto cried out,
"I'm lucky the cops caught me!"

---

*   Traditional Mexican song sung while hitting the piñata.

BREATH OF LIFE

We can breathe once again.
Open the windows!
We are no longer frozen by fear.
Open the windows!
We can sleep tight now.
Open the windows!

No more Night Stalker,
only summer night breezes.
We can breathe once more!

Sacred Sam

Southern Brother Sam,
hermano de ceremonia,
sits in sweats and sings his songs.

Southern Brother Sam
solidarily* sits through my sad and salty tears
as we listen to *Sor Juana Inés de la Cruz.*

Southern Brother Sam
quietly sits, soothing my broken soul
while holding sacred space in solemn silence.

---

*   Solidarily is a new adverb to describe how one sits in solidarity, created just for this poem!

I Think I Was Born Angry

They say that a woman's ovum develop
while in the womb of their mothers.

My great grandmother was nine months pregnant
and busting her back as a farmworker,
giving birth to my grandmother
in the middle of the barley fields of *Santa Monica.*

They say that a woman's ovum develop
while in the womb of their mothers.

My grandmother spent her entire pregnancy
working from dawn to dusk
while my grandfather drank from dusk to dawn,
not coming home until she went and dragged him out of the bars.

They say that a woman's ovum develop
while in the womb of their mothers.

For forty weeks of gestation,
my mother swallowed daily doses of tears
alongside her morning coffee,
wanting to run back home every second of the day.

They say that a woman's ovum develop
while in the womb of their mothers.

It was I who was angry in the 1920's.
It was I who was angry in the 1950's.
It was I who was angry in the 1970's.

And it was I who was still angry in the 1990's
while giving birth to a beautiful baby boy,
the one who came to finally put an end to this generational curse.

A River Runs Through Us

A river of tears, sweat, and blood.

A river filled with fears and murky mud.

An overflowing river of light and love.

A symmetrical reflection—as below, so above.

AHÍ LOS VIDRIOS

La ventana delantera de mi carro se astilló
con tal de ya no manejar por tu calle.

El vidrio de mis espejuelos se rayó
para no tener que mirar aquellos, tus ojos.

Las copas de cristal se estrellaron
pues nunca más querrán tocar tus labios.

Los espejos del lavabo se salpicaron,
jamás volverán a ser testigos de tu presencia.

La ventana de la sala se agujeró,
despidiendo de mi casa tu esencia,

y así, con los vientos de Santa Ana,
trayendo nuevos aires a mi hogar.

EASTWARD

EXPANSION

A Horse With No Name

GLITTER AND GLISTEN

See how the sun sparkles softly over the salt water,
how the pitter-patter of perspiration peeks through peoples' pores,
how soft summer sands sift through sinking city toes,
how motors race through rip currents releasing giant ripples,
how brown desert hills bustle with boisterous brown bodies,
while wistful palm trees wave with the wind
on the other side of the hills.

Winds of Change

As I drove through the valley of Mystic Lake,
I pondered on my life as an ever-moving Libra.
Suddenly, the winds rushed in,
moving the giant, ancient trees.
So moved were they,
that they bowed as I drove up,
waving goodbye as I drove past.

MONSOON

I left my steady blues skies
for the tumultuous thunders of your love.
Your walloping winds carried me away
while your rapid rains flooded my barren canyons.
Then, when monsoon season was over, so were we.

DESIERTO

She had the most unusual name, different, but befitting. Her name was *Desierto*, which in English means desert. He had met her through a family friend, and like a magnet, he instantly clung to her, holding on for dear life. Although he thought he had fallen in love, he merely suffered from some hypnotic intoxication of some sort. He fooled himself into believing the carelessly-created-mirage of his mind.

Desierto's extreme emotions controlled the climate of her life; hers, as well as those in her proximity. Days came when her passions exceeded 120F, yet times of near-frostbite chills also permeated her existence. Although some thought of her as a wasteland, he witnessed the abundant miracles that flourished around her, which only strengthened the intoxicating trance.

Her cacti never appeared parched, despite her endlessly supplying him with her waters of life. He pushed her love to the limits, yet she endured the droughts. Her reptiles possessed the power to shed the old, while the Northern winds blew away the tragic past. Sadly, he lacked her same capacity to release, and hence, continually stomped on her serpent ways. Every night, her resilient lizards maintained the ability to survive below-zero heartache. Every morning, she prayed for the sun to melt the nightly ice sculptures he created. Despite the blazing acclamations of her amazing abilities, he proved unable to comprehend her magic. All the while, he beheld her talents in incomprehensible awe. The more he partook of her *jícuri*, the deeper he fell into a mind-altering spell.

Although this girl was a desert, she was not deserted. Allured by her magnetism, many organized pilgrimages to her lands. Like tumbleweed, only those able to withstand extremes managed to thrive, for a while, at least. To his misfortune, he could not handle the intensity found in *Desierto*. Ignorantly, he imagined that *Desierto* would live a life of solitude. His attempts to wipe out her existence became futile. Exhausted and dehydrated, he chose abandonment, holding in one hand, the disintegrating image of his man-made mirage.

Uto-Aztecan

Adobe: In the Beginning

Her walls were so thick,
it took years for her to finally see him.
Like the ancient walls of *Casa Grande*,
he eventually wore her down,
breaking through what seemed impossibly impenetrable.
And like the great peoples of that Southwestern region,
one day, he just disappeared,
leaving her in ruins.

Adobe: In the End

What people see as the Ruins of *Casa Grande*,
she sees as resilience.
When people chipped away and tore down her walls,
she stood, immovable and anchored in time and history.
When people abandoned her,
leaving her alone and unprotected,
she communed with her ancestors from a time long before.
When people saw her as ruins,
she saw herself as indestructible,
whispering to the winds,
"And still, I stand!"

LAND OF THE TSALAGI

Enraged Red Woman

I am a red woman who is enraged.

I am appalled to be living in the 21st Century
where I seem to be stuck within the confines
of the Twilight Zone.

I am angered at the lack of consciousness throughout humanity
where breathing is impossible within the confines
of a deteriorated ozone.

I am infuriated with society's prevalence of misogynistic terrorism
where my body is trapped within the confines
of a patriarchal war zone.

The reels of human evolution have been switched into reverse
because the issues that haunted my ancestors still haunt me today!

I am not a misandrist! By no means a bigot or hater.
I am not a misanthrope for I love each and every neighbor.

I am simply an enraged red woman
who is sick and tired of being enraged.

GIGAGE

Red is the blood that boils within my veins.
Red are the murdered and missing.
Red is the lipstick he sees as slut.
Red are my eyes filled with rage.
Red is the war paint tattooed on my skin.
Red are the hands of every broken treaty.
Red is my bloody moon that reminds me:
I am The-Giver-of-Life!

A Land Where the Brave Have Never Truly Been Free

Some people say that there is no room for abortion in this country,
that "we" are a "God-fearing nation"
that would **NEVER** endanger a child.

THIS, the same country that stripped children
away from their families,
their languages, their cultures.

THIS, the same country that gloats of religious freedom
while strategically dismantling
the spiritual posterity
of the original inhabitants'
future generations.

THIS, the same country that shipped
little boys and girls off to boarding schools,
thousands of miles away from home,
schools designed to
"kill the Indian, save the man."

THIS, the same country that did,
in fact, kill
"One little, two little, three little Indians…"
with a count that has never ceased.

THIS, the same country that boasts of a
Statue of Liberty who
"lifts (her) lamp beside the Golden Door."
Yet as Shakespeare warns:
"All that glitters is not gold."

THIS, the same country whose golden door
is but a mere steel gate,
entryway and terminal to endless rows of cages
atop **I.C.E.** cold slabs of cement and dirt floors.

THIS, the same country holding hostage
"huddled (brown) masses
(wrapped in foil blankets)
yearning to be free."

THIS, the same country that claims to be
the "land of the free, home of the brave."
THIS, a land where the brave have never truly been free.

THE

WANDERER

Ni de aquí, ni de allá

Fish Out of Water

Flip! Flop!
Flip! Flop!
Stop!
Tic-toc! Tic-toc!
One turns into two.
Two turns into three.
Three turns into a flock
of sheep
jumping over the clock.
And all of my thoughts...
Tic-toc!
Incessantly, they stalk.
Tic-tock!
My sleep.
Flip-flop! Flip-flop!
There's a mermaid on the dock
who desires to swim, but forgot.
Now, finds herself terribly distraught.
Flip-flop! Flip-flop!
Marco Polo always sought
to seek
trying to beat
the clock.
Tic-tock! Tic-tock!
Fish out of water.
Flip! Flop!
Flip! Flop!

One mariposita que Try to Fly

Some people insist on being rooted,
yet not all of us are trees.
Others insist we grasp the ground,
when there are those of us who have wings.
Creepy crawlers know one thing,
to creep and crawl the Earth.
There are those of us who fly through skies,
been doing so since birth.

I was born in L.A. County.
Raised in the great O.C.
I've roamed through the counties of Riverside
and the ginormous SBC.
I jumped across the border
to reconnect with my *Chicali* roots.
My earthly regalia runs the gambit:
from ribbon skirts to classic suits.

The *P'urhépecha mariposa*
makes every corner her home.
I, too, am a *Tzintzun*
meant to roam and roam.
Yet some people still insist,
trying so hard to root down my ME.
I, too, am a butterfly,
flying high and flying free.

Illegal

"That which we call a rose
by any other name would smell as sweet."
- William Shakespeare

I smell of sweet grass and sage,
copal and *palo santo.*

White feathers.
Brown feathers.
Black feathers and gray.

I smell of *ruda* and *hierbabuena,*
bear grease and lavender.

Sahumerios.
White candles.
Smudging shells and sticks.

I smell of *osha* and tobacco,
alcohol preparado.

Ribbon skirts.
Fringed shawls.
Cowboy boots and buckles.

I smell of *jícuri* and *yagé,*
incense and smoke.

Rebozos.
Long braids.
Rattles and drums.

I smell of contrived controversy.

No Dawes Rolls.
No tribal I.D.
No indigenous clan for me.

I smell of contrived controversy.

My life,
my labels,
my medicines,
my homelands

undocumented and unafraid!

THIS LAND IS MY LAND

WHO'S THAT GIRL?

¿Que quién soy y adónde voy?[*]
I am *Citlali*, a speckle of stardust
that sparkles under the sun.

But, where are you from? Where are you from?
Soy de un mundo de las estrellas del mucho más allá.
Adriana la Xicana proviene de Andrómeda.

¿Y por qué vivo en una bóveda?
Soy hija de la luna, hija del Mictlán,
hija del inframundo y las cavernas de Teotihuacán.
Soy una itzcuintli de Xolotl.

¿Entonces, cuál es tu complot?
Recordar. Recordar. Recordar.

Yo vine a este mundo a recopilar.
My life from *Atl'antix*, purple mountains, and *Tulúm*
My life as love-making *Diosa* and as *tochtli* on the moon.
My time as *sacerdotisa*; my time as slave.
My time as *caballero*, my time as knave.

I am…
commander-in-chief of a nave big and wide
with my trusted *copiloto*, Cutie-Q, by my side.

Yo soy…
guardiana de una calavera, Hun-Tijax is her sacred name.
A rainbow obsidian crystal skull *camina conmigo* as I regain…

Memoria. Memoria. Memoria.
Who am I? Where am I from?
¿Cuál es mi triste historia?

---

[*]   This poem first appeared in in the Rio Grande Valley International Poetry Festival's Anthology, *Boundless*, 2023.

¿Triste mi historia? ¡Nada de eso!
Aunque a mi no me han regalado
ni siquiera un solo hueso.

¿A qué viene todo esto?
Trasmutar. Trasmutar. Trasmutar.

Yo vine a este mundo a sanar
el ataque a mi chakra vocal,
y los traumas que giran en el gran espiral.

¿A qué viniste sagrada nahual?
Amar. Amar. Amar.

The physical matter does not matter.
Geography is just a place.
Who I am and where I'm from
is just a 3D chase.
Solo se que vine a aprender
how to love this human race.
Who's that girl? *Es la pregunta* that many want to know.
Not just where I came from, but where I want to go.
Only this, I know...

Soy, doy, vengo y voy.
Un recuerdo. Una memoria. Una recopilación.
Un misterio. Una historia. Una fuerte trasmutación.
Desenvoltura. Desentierro. Una gran revolución.
Convocatoria. Gran silencio. Sagrada sanación.

Ella es...
Nosotr@s somos...
Amor. Amor. Amor.

LA GRAN MANIFESTACIÓN

Amo a to'
(Matarilerileron)

¿Qué quiere usted?
(Matarilerileron)

Yo quiero paz.
(Matarilerileron)

Yo quiero equidad.
(Matarilerileron)

Yo no quiero la violencia.
(Matarilerileron)

Lo que quiero es la justicia.
(Matarilerileron)

Ese juicio sí me agrada.
(Matarilerileron)

Porque tú eres mi hermana.

(Matarilerileron)

Porque tú eres mi hermano.

(Matarilerileron)

Démonos tod@s la mano.

(Matarilerileron)

De este pan tod@s comemos.

(Matarilerileron)

Casa a tod@s les pondremos.

(Matarilerileron)

Ese juicio sí me agrada.

(Matarilerileron)

Porque yo se que me amas.

(Matarilerileron)

Porque yo también te amo.

(Matarilerileron)

Nuestro mundo es sagrado.

(Matarilerileron)*

-Amor a tod@s . . .

---

*   This poem was inspired by the classic children's song in Spanish, *Amo Ato.*

DEDICATED TO
THE ORIGINAL INHABITANTS
OF ALL THE PLACES MENTIONED
& MY PEEPS FROM A VALLEY UNKNOWN.

XOXO,

DIOSA X

ABOUT THE AUTHOR

Diosa Xochiquetzalcóatl, or Diosa X for short, is a multilingual and multidimensional Xicana, Indigenous, MeXicana poetiza. She is a seasoned language arts educator with a Bachelor's in English and a Master's in Cross-Cultural Education, as well as a Level 1 Kundalini Yoga Instructor and a student of Nahualísmo. Diosa X has been writing since her preteen years, first publishing her poems in her high school's bilingual literary magazine, Las Voces. But it wasn't until adulthood that she began to participate in open mics at Tia Chuchas and Tonalli Studios; and it was then that she recommitted to her poetry and finally embraced her life as a poet, and eventually, author.

In 2022, Diosa participated and won Chicago's only Spanish-language slam, Slam Diáspora, which sent her, in partnership with the Fiesta Literaria de las Periferias (FLUP) to the continental tournament, Abya Yala: Copa América de Poetry Slam in Rio de Janeiro, Brazil. Prior to this experience, she also competed in the 2017 CABE Conference Spoken Word Competition, tying for first. Most recently, Diosa X became the Rio Grande Valley International Poetry Festival's first slam champion in 2023.

This poet has facilitated poetry workshops in English, Spanish, and bilingually for the Sims Library/Los Angeles Public Library's Adult Literacy Program; Tumblewords Project; Contracorriente: Cruce de poesía y transgresión, a binational women writers retreat in Ixtapa, Mexico; Ovitt Library in the city of Ontario; the Rio Grande Valley International Poetry Festival; and the La Raza Youth Empowerment Conference at LA Mission College.

Diosa Xochiquetzalcóatl is a proud member of the international women's poetry troupe, Tesoro at https://firesingers.com/; California Poets in the Schools as a teacher-in-training at https://www.californiapoets.org/; Circulo de poetas and Writers at https://circulowriters.com/, CABE; and Inlandia.

A Note from the Publisher

This book would not be possible without the generous support of Nervous Ghost Press, Matthew Mejia, and the Community Arts Workspace where this book took shape. Thank you!

Mil gracias...Tlazocamati a T'sanda Janini por la portada tán hermosa creada especialmente para este libro. Many thanks to the book cover artist for her beautiful work gracing the cover.
Find and follow her on Instagram @tsanda_ink_; Facebook at T'sanda Janini; or TikTok @Tsandaink.

Riot of Roses Publishing House was founded in 2021 specifically to amplify the stories of historically silenced voices.

Xicana owned. Mujerista focused. For the people.

We publish books to heal and liberate others.

Read our rebellion.

www.riotofrosespublishinghouse.com

RIOT OF ROSES
PUBLISHING HOUSE

SEJATNGA
UNCEDED TONGVA TERRITORY
SOUTH WHITTIER, CALIFORNIA